I HAVE THE POWER TO GROW
Affirmations for Young & Old

Miah

Bodi

Riley

Addy

Building a foundation for positive thoughts.

**Written & Illustrated By:
Faith Spencer, RMT, PhD**

I HAVE THE POWER TO GROW
Affirmations for Young and Old

Written & Illustrated by Faith Spencer RMT, PhD

Published by
Joshua Tree Publishing
• Chicago •
JoshuaTreePublishing.com

All rights reserved. No part of this book may be reproduced or transmitted in any form or by any means, electronic or mechanical, including information storage and retrieval system without written permission from the publisher, except by a reviewer who may quote brief passages in a review.

13-Digit ISBN: 978-1-941049-91-4
Copyright © 2018. Faith Spencer, RMT, PhD All Rights Reserved.

Disclaimer:

The information given in this book is not intended to act as a substitute for medical treatment, nor can it be used instead of mental health options. If you feel that you or your child need further help, please contact your medical doctor or call your local mental health provider.

The affirmations are to be a positive in your life and the life of the child you are reading this to. This book should never be used as a substitute—if deeper help is needed please be proactive and call for help. You have the POWER to make a POSITIVE change in your life.

It is my hope that you will continue your own understanding in natural therapies and how they can work hand in hand with western medicine.

This book is designed to provide information about the subject matter covered. The opinions and information expressed in this book are those of the author, not the publisher. The author and publisher of this book shall have neither liability nor responsibility to any person or entity with respect to any loss or damage caused or alleged to be caused directly or indirectly by the information contained in this book.

Printed in the United States of America

DEDICATION

To the young and old looking to make a positive change in this world.

To all of the children reading this book or having someone read it to you,
YOU ARE STRONG, YOU ARE IMPORTANT,
and YOU CAN BE ANYTHING YOU DESIRE!

To my little friend who has inspired
me to write more, thank you Adisyn.

> ### TO MY CHILDREN
> Ashley, Blake, Jeremiah and Sean . . . I love you all so much.
> No matter where you are in the world I am with you.
> You each have such beauty inside you, and I hope
> you never let anyone take that away from you.
>
> LOVE MOM!

ACKNOWLEDGEMENTS

MOM AND DAD YOU HAVE ALWAYS TOLD ME
THAT I CAN DO ANYTHING!
Thank you both for always answering the phone
and keeping me full of JOY, INSPIRATION & HOPE.

Nancy, Linda, and John thank you for the love and support.
Nancy you always have the best coffee and make everyday
a day full of love and smiles. Thank you for taking my son
and I into your home and being a positive in our lives.

T.J.H thank you for the support talks and time you
took to read and re-read all of my books!

Those around me who I call my TRIBE . . .
Thank you for keeping our little world running so that
I can write and I can discover my passions.

Joe you have left this world, but you
still inspire me to do good. It is the stories that are told about you
that make me want to be as selfless as you were.

I believe that I am a kind and loving person.

I am able to forgive.

I can forgive myself and understand no one is perfect.

I am the only one who has the power over me.

I can accept my individuality.

I AM KIND.

I am capable of anything I set my mind to.

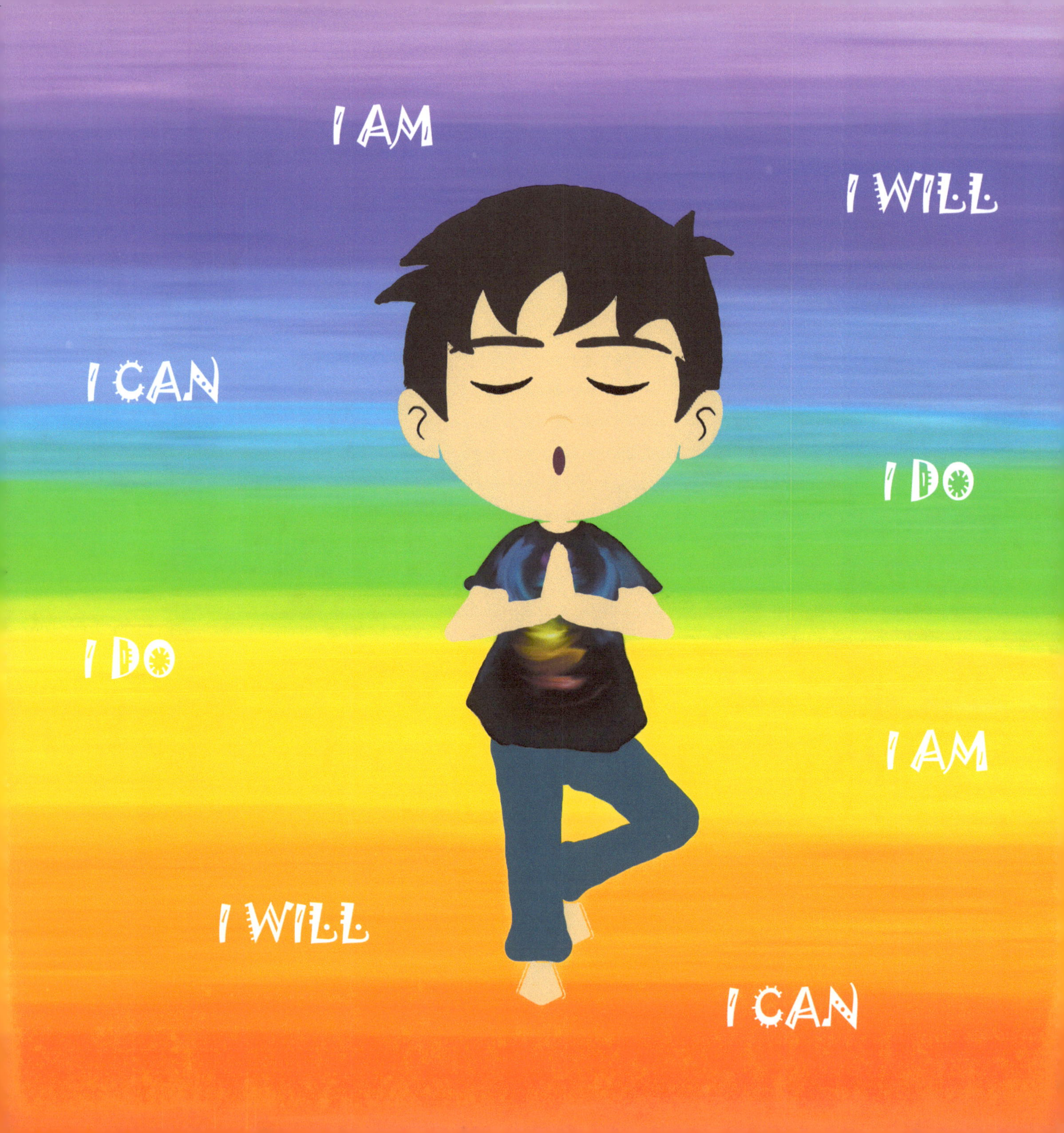
I AM
I WILL
I CAN
I DO
I DO
I AM
I WILL
I CAN

I have the power to GROW

About the Author

Faith Spencer, RMT, PhD has worked with people young and old across America to build positive foundations for everyone who would like to make a change. Faith takes being a Personal Life Coach to the next level with working as a family. She takes families on a journey together to rebuild healthy bonds and relationships.

As a mother of 4 amazing children she understands the importance of living what you wish others to live. She reads her books to her son Sean Riley and does positive affirmations with him daily. She believes that children should have positive power given to them and that they take on what they hear.
SO WHY NOT BUILD THEM UP WITH EMPOWERMENT AND POSITIVITY.

Faith has been a Holistic Health Practitioner for over 20 years and has had wellness studios in San Diego, CA - Maui, HI - North Carolina and now is based out of Joshua Tree, CA.

Instagram @DustyPawsRanch
Facebook @OmniRejuvenationWellnessStudio

www.ingramcontent.com/pod-product-compliance
Lightning Source LLC
Chambersburg PA
CBHW050750110526
44591CB00002B/36